Aspiration

Birmingham's
Historic Houses of Worship

ORIGINAL LIMITED EDITION
Copyright 2000

Birmingham Historical Society
One Sloss Quarters, Birmingham, Alabama 35222
Telephone 205-251-1880. Faximile 205-251-3260.
Website: www. bhistorical.org

Birmingham Historical Society is a private, non-profit organization whose mission is
to contribute to the quality of life in Birmingham by preserving, learning from and
celebrating the city's past while helping to shape its future.

Design Scott Fuller

Readers: Alice Bowsher, Lee Brewer, Ronda Chambless, Elizabeth Collier, Rhonda Covington,
Cathy Dodds, Jim Emison, Leah Harris, Barbara Schnorrenberg, Joe Strickland

Library of Congress 00 133209
ISBN 0-943994-26-8

Cover Illustrations: Front: *left to right*, First United Methodist Church of Birmingham, Temple Emanu-El,
First Presyterian Church, The Cathedral of St. Paul, Highlands United Methodist Church.
Back: First United Methodist Church of Birmingham

Aspiration

Birmingham's Historic Houses of Worship

John M. Schnorrenberg

Photographs by Richard Payne

Edited by Philip A. Morris, Marjorie L. White

Birmingham Historical Society

with the support of

ARCHANGELS

Mr. & Mrs. Herbert E. Longnecker, Robert R. Meyer Foundation
Susan Mott Webb Charitable Trust

ANGELS

Mr. & Mrs. Thomas M. Boulware, Mr. & Mrs. Ehney A. Camp, III
The Daniel Foundation of Alabama, Mr. & Mrs. D. Lawrence Faulkner
Mr. & Mrs. James M. S. French, Mr. & Mrs. Wyatt R. Haskell
Mr. & Mrs. Thomas H. Lowder, Mr. Henry S. Lynn Jr., Mr. & Mrs. William M. Spencer III
Mr. & Mrs. Arnold L. Steiner, Mr. & Mrs. Hall W. Thompson, Mr. & Mrs. James H. White III

CHERUBS

Mr & Mrs. Richard A. Bowron, Mr. & Mrs. Charles S. Caldwell III
Mr. & Mrs. Jeffrey H. Cohn, Mr. Egar B. Marx, Jr., Mr. James D. Sokol

Foreword

Visitors exposed to Birmingham's downtown and the city's early neighborhoods often remark on the number of substantial and architecturally distinguished houses of worship that punctuate the urban landscape.

Next to towering modern office buildings, the human scale, rich textures and intimate courtyards of late 19th and early 20th century churches provide dramatic contrast. At Five Points South and nearby along Highland Avenue, prominent churches and synagogues anchor a lively, changing scene with a sense of civic importance and durability. And deep within residential districts, religious structures with their lofty porticoes or steeples maintain the skyline dominance once common to all towns and cities.

Under the sponsorship of the Birmingham Historical Society, many Birmingham residents have enjoyed learning about our religious architecture through Dr. John Schnorrenberg's annual Palm Sunday tours conducted over the past 16 seasons. Some will recall him bringing home a point about the acoustics of pre-amplification sanctuaries by suddenly raising his voice to booming preacher volume, or noting that an original layout that called for church members to enter with the congregation facing them sometime later was reversed — the latecomers' salvation, it might be construed.

For many years, we have wished to have John's informative commentary combined with fine photography in a permanent, accessible form — namely, a book. *ASPIRATION* is that wish fulfilled.

We started making lists of worthy candidates, and, given our embarrassment of riches, they got quite long. Not wanting to produce a catalogue of small images that would miss the scope and richness of the subject matter, the book evolved into a limited number of sites that could be rather lavishly displayed. And because those built from the late 19th century up to about World War II represented an eclectic but coherent period (and one during which the structures relate to surrounding contexts rather than loosely placed amid parking areas), we concentrate on this period.

We began discussing the project with Richard Payne, FAIA, an architectural photographer based in Houston who has leading architecture firms as clients, but who also relishes the chance to show how buildings shape the character of a whole town or city. He recommended black and white to give the book distinction and illuminate the light, shadow and form of buildings. When he made the first of several visits to begin doing the work, the stained glass changed his mind: We needed a segment in color to do it justice.

Payne came alone, and largely worked solo, as is his wont, on three week-long visits and a shorter stay to make his photographs. We asked him to capture the individual buildings, but to also have some views give a larger sense of context. So the book also gives some sense of the larger city while staying focused on its subjects.

We were pleased when we started seeing the prints Payne produced in his Houston studio. And when graphic artist Scott Fuller began running printouts of pages at the scale of the book, with many images sweeping across two pages, we were even more excited. The photographer established up-front that his photographs were not to be cropped, but he worked with Fuller on the format, so there was a good fit. When it came to the cover, the desire was to have a selection, not a single edifice. Vertical slices seemed better at signaling both the variety and scope of what lay inside. Payne approved the idea. Fuller did a fine job of selecting the views and deftly bounding and separating the black and white images with color to make the design whole.

Since the purpose of the book is to fully portray the architecture and to benefit from John's informed description and analysis, the text freely employs words and terms that many people don't regularly encounter. A glossary is provided for handy reference.

So, here we are, at last, with the pleasure of touring Birmingham's notable religious landmarks illuminated by intelligent commentary and allowed to linger as long as desired. It is, simultaneously, a portrait of determined vision, architectural talent, fine craft, earnest fund-raising, generous giving and, finally, that of a city blessed with religious aspiration translated into art.

Philip A. Morris, Marjorie L. White

Introduction

The architectural history of the churches and synagogues of Birmingham is the story this book tells in pictures and in words. It is told only for the city's first hundred years, 1871 to 1971, and the emphasis in that century is on the buildings designed between 1886 and 1930, a span of just 44 years. The photographs and descriptions are intended to be a report on churches and synagogues that still exist and are still in use for worship, although not always by the denominations which first built them. The many buildings built and used before 1886 are all destroyed, and many built since then have been destroyed or put to secular use. In 1972 there were 606 churches and synagogues listed in the Birmingham city directory. ASPIRATION illustrates and briefly describes only 37 of these buildings. Some are as small and as simple as Thomas Presbyterian (1891), *right**; others are more elaborate like the First Methodist Church of Ensley (1910), *below*.

Why has Birmingham aspired to build so many places of worship? These places listed in the 1972 city directory are those existing in 1971. If one divides their number into the 1970 census population of the city (305,983), there were 505 persons for each church then. The population of the city had declined from its

Thomas Baptist Church-Old Thomas Presbyterian Church (1891).

1950 size (326,037), but there were still enough worshipers to justify all those buildings. Churches and synagogues are built because of the need to accommodate their congregations and in hope of further growth.

Neighborhoods

Where are the city's churches and synagogues? They have always stood where her people dwelled, and that is true even of the oldest structures. Four of these buildings had been built on Sixth Avenue North by 1911: the First Baptist at Twenty-second Street (1902), the Church of the Advent at Twentieth Street (1887), the First Methodist at Nineteenth Street (1890), and Sixteenth Street Baptist at Sixteenth Street (1909). Sixth Avenue and the blocks just north and south of it were still a major residential area. (Fifth Avenue was considered the finest residential address of the late nineteenth century.) Sixth Avenue bordered on the edges of two of the three downtown parks. These parks were surrounded by houses, many of them the residences of prosperous white citizens, those closer to Sixteenth Street Baptist the houses of Jewish and black residents. Even in the 1920s, this row of churches increased by the addition of Sixth Avenue Presbyterian Church (1925) at Eighteenth Street. Close to Sixth Avenue are The Cathedral of St. Paul, at Third Avenue and Twenty-second Street (1890), and the oldest surviving church, First Presbyterian, at Fourth Avenue and Twenty-first

Soul's Harbor Deliverance Center-Old Ensley First United Methodist Church (1910).

* Dates given in the Introduction are those when construction began.

Harmony Street Baptist Church (1924), architect: Wallace A. Rayfield.

(1888). The first Temple Emanu-El (1886) stood on Fifth Avenue next to Kelly Ingram Park. On the other side of Sixth Avenue, Knesseth Israel built its temple in 1908 at Seventh and Eighteenth Street. Simpson Methodist Church was built at Seventh Avenue and Twenty-third Street in 1903, and the First Christian Church built its Education Building on Twenty-first Street just beyond Seventh Avenue, in 1924, adding the church as late as 1957.

Five Points South

A second group of churches and synagogues at the center of a residential community are those at or near Five Points Circle, the central intersection of the early suburban town of Highland. St. Mary's-on-the-Highlands built its first church on this circle (1887) and then moved only a couple of blocks away to Twelfth Avenue South at Nineteenth Street (1891). Highland Avenue

Central Park Missionary Baptist Church-Old Central Park Presbyterian Church (1926, 1948), architects: George P. Turner; Van Keuren, Davis & Co..

continues the line of Twelfth Avenue across Twentieth Street. South Highland Presbyterian (1891) and Temple Emanu-El (1911) are across Highland from each other at Twenty-first Street, and Temple Beth-El (1926) is only a few blocks further along Highland. Eleventh Avenue South intersects Twentieth Street at the Five Points Circle, and here the Methodists built Highlands Methodist (1907). The Baptists located Southside Baptist at Eleventh Avenue and Nineteenth Street (1910), just one block down the hill from St. Mary's and within sight of Highlands Methodist Church. Many homes surrounded these churches.

Highland-Southside

Highland was the town of the prosperous. Only a few blocks west of it on Tenth and Eleventh Avenues South, a neighborhood of middle-class people built their community of churches just after 1900. Second Presbyterian rose on Tenth Avenue South at Twelfth Street (1901), Eleventh Avenue Methodist on Twelfth Street at Eleventh Avenue (1902), and St. Andrew's Episcopal Church (1913) just across Twelfth from the Methodists. These three buildings are within sight of one another. Only a few blocks west of them are two ethnic Catholic churches, St. Elias Maronite Church (1945) and St. George Melkite Church (1959). Both are close to the extension of Tenth Avenue South. St. Elias is on Eighth Street and St. George on Fifth Street. They serve the neigborhood in which their people came to live.

St. Elias and St. George moved south and west from their original sites at Sixth Avenue South and Twentieth Street, and Ninth Avenue South and Thirteenth, respectively. Their shift was part of the abandoning of the inner Southside by many small churches. Southside Baptist moved from its second location at Seventh Avenue South and Twentieth Street. Only two major white churches remain, Third Presbyterian (1902) at Seventh Avenue and Twenty-first Street, and Holy Trinity-Holy Cross Cathedral (1949) at Third Avenue South and Nineteenth Street. The present cathedral replaced an early Methodist church on that site, which Holy Trinity acquired in 1906. Major black churches of inner Southside still standing are Twenty-third Street Baptist (1929), designed by L. H. Persley, and Thirty-second Street Baptist (1924) by Wallace Rayfield, both black architects. Small black churches still pepper neighboring streets. Once these churches were surrounded by the mill houses of the worker-tenants who attended them.

Avondale-Woodlawn-East Lake

Other church groups built in new residential areas of expanding Birmingham to the east of the central city. In historically white Avondale are South Avondale

Baptist (1914) and Avondale Methodist (1931), the two survivors of others built before 1971, *pages 5 & 7.* They are only a couple of blocks apart. Historically black North Avondale has Harmony Street Baptist (1924) and St. James A.M.E. (1929) across the street from each other, *page 2.* Further out are the churches of Woodlawn where Baptists, Methodists, Presbyterians and Episcopalians had principal churches, built within sight of one another on First Avenue North. Still further out are the numerous churches of East Lake, many of them along Division Avenue and First and Second Avenues South. East Lake United Methodist Church (1945) and Ruhama Baptist Church (1923) are two of these.

West End and Ensley

Churches west of the central city also rose to serve their neighborhoods. There are dozens of churches in West End, a number of them on or close to Pearson Avenue where Blessed Sacrament Catholic Church (1928) still stands and is in use. Another is Walker Memorial Methodist on Tuscaloosa Avenue (1918), and there are several other churches within a few blocks of it. But the West End churches are scattered through the vast territory of its multitude of houses. They are incidents, not a collective focus. Ensley has a downtown, and a number of churches stand close to that now mostly abandoned business district and the former streetcar lines. They are with the homes of their people, but they also stand near the center of that industrial city. This book examines only four Ensley churches: St. Joseph's Catholic Church (1914) in the former Little Italy neighborhood, Macedonia Missionary Baptist Church (1965), First United Methodist Church of Ensley (1910), and the extraordinary Ensley Baptist Church (1928). Further west than Ensley is Central Park. Its principal churches string along or near the old Bessemer streetcar line and superhighway. These survivors are an extraordinary group including Hunter Street Baptist (1927, 1956), Central Park Presbyterian (1926), *page 2,* and Central Park Baptist (1952).

Perhaps this book neglects North Birmingham, but it takes a glimpse at North Avondale and pays a visit to Fountain Heights, looking at one of its numerous churches, the fine building erected for Calvary Baptist Church (1922), *above.*

Southern Suburbs

A few churches in the present suburbs of Birmingham are included. Trinity United Methodist Church in Homewood is a campus of four church buildings, erected from 1927 to 1976, *right.* Trinity was founded in 1891 in Birmingham's Southside neighborhood at Sixth Avenue and Thirtieth Street, moved in 1909 to

Interior, Macedonia Seventeenth Street Baptist Church-Old Calvary Baptist Church (1922), architect: J. E. Green.

Clairmont Avenue, and then went to the new suburb of Homewood in the 1920s. Canterbury United Methodist Church (1961) is included to represent the numerous churches of Mountain Brook, *page 4.* Canterbury demonstrates a change of location different from that of Trinity. It united two country churches: one of 1874, replaced in 1896 and remodeled in 1928 (Union Hill Church); the other which built its first church in 1912. That frame building still stands as the Steeple Arts Academy in Crestline Village. As in the city, so in the suburbs: churches go where people are.

Architectural Styles and Designers

The art historian describes, defines and analyzes style. Style is appearance classified to give it a recognizable

Right to left, Meeting Hall, Educational Building (1927) and Sanctuary (1949), Trinity United Methodist Church, architect: Warren, Knight & Davis.

Canterbury United Methodist Church (1961), architect: Shaw and Renneker.

face. Churches have styles, and most churches of the nineteenth and twentieth centuries are built in one or another of the styles which revived earlier historic styles. Architects are the style makers and stylists.

Gothic Style

The Gothic style first appears in a surviving Birmingham church in First Presbyterian, said to have been the design of a New York architect. The nineteenth-century Gothic of First Presbyterian, Advent, St. Paul's, St. Mary's, and South Highland Presbyterian Church is not so historically correct in detail as Warren and Knight's Independent Presbyterian (or even John Marriott's St. Andrew's), but this earlier Gothic reflects the achievements of nationally important architects such as James Renwick (1818-1895) and J. Wrey Mould (1825-1886). Renwick designed the original Smithsonian Institution in Washington (1847-1855) and St. Patrick's Cathedral in New York (1858-1879, 1886-1887). Mould, who was born and trained in England, was the architect of Trinity Parish School (1860) and one of the architects of the Museum of Natural History (1874-1877), both in New York, as well as of a number of churches. He used the English High Victorian Gothic style in his church buildings and introduced architectural polychromy to the United States. First Presbyterian, St. Paul's, and South Highland Presbyterian reflect Mould and Renwick's influence.

Adolphus Druiding (1839-1899), the architect of St. Paul's, was German born and trained and brought with him to the United States the knowledge of German Gothic and the German Gothic Revival which shapes the style of his numerous church buildings and of St.

Paul's. Druiding's career was in the Middle West, rather than in the Eastern United States like Renwick and Mould. John Marriott (1879-1958), architect of Neo-Gothic St. Andrew's Episcopal Church in Birmingham, finished his education at the University of Illinois in 1904, and practiced in the city from 1913 to 1916. Like William Weston and Druiding, Marriott came to Birmingham from the Middle West. That is true of Charles and Harry Wheelock also. Charles Wheelock (1833-1910), first trained as a carpenter in upstate New York, came to Birmingham in 1881 via Kansas, New Mexico, and Texas. His Church of the Advent was designed in an elaborately adorned and decorated Gothic Revival style but built far more simply. The Advent shares its simplification with St. Mary's, designed by John Sutcliffe (1853-1913), who came to Birmingham from England and practiced here from 1886 to 1892. These churches are a plainer and more severe reductionist Gothic than First Presbyterian.

Romanesque Style

But there are other important revival styles, and in young Birmingham one of the most influential was the Romanesque Revival, the style of the First Methodist Church of Birmingham by Weary and Kramer of Akron, Ohio. This 1890 building is the up-to-date response to H. H. Richardson's (1836-1886) Trinity Church Boston of 1873, the defining example of Romanesque Revival style which is sometimes called Richardsonian Romanesque or American Romanesque. The Romanesque of Richardson is echoed finely by George Kramer's great church, but there are numerous American Romanesque buildings in Birmingham: First Methodist of Ensley (1910) and First Methodist of Woodlawn (1909) among them. Indeed, Romanesque architectural concepts are developed in two important later Birmingham churches. The first building that Warren, Knight & Davis did for Trinity Church in Homewood in 1927 was both church and church school, *page 3*. The entrance door is framed in a two-story high semicircular arch of three receding orders, the inner two with medievalizing Corinthianesque capitals. These forms and the window arches give a Romanesque effect. The last major Romanesque design in Birmingham is East Lake United Methodist Church, built from 1945 to 1948 from the design of George P. Turner (1896-1984) of Turner and Batson. Turner was born in Birmingham and came back to practice in 1925. Turner's Romanesque is actually more Italian Lombard in style and not derived, as is Richardsonian Romanesque, from French and Spanish sources. It is also more archaeological in some of its exactitudes than the freer expressions of Richardson or the simplifications of his followers.

Trade Journals

What helps make the various architectural styles of Birmingham churches possible are the architectural magazines which begin publication just after Birmingham was founded in 1871. *The American Architect and Building News* began in 1876. *The Archtectural Record* first appeared in 1891. Every architectural practitioner subscribed to these journals, and many bound and kept them. The bound volumes of the *American Architect and Building News* in the library at Auburn University were the gift of Harry Wheelock (1866-1940), son and partner of his father Charles Wheelock. These have binders' labels in them which show that they were bound in Birmingham during Wheelock's lifetime and presumably for his use. So both local and visiting architects who designed the churches of Birmingham shared the architectural knowledge that the new well-illustrated publications gave to all. Birmingham churches were published in American architectural magazines. George Kramer (1847-1938) published First Methodist, Birmingham, in the *Inland Architect and News Record*, vol. 16 (before 1891). Warren, Knight & Davis published their buildings, including Independent Presbyterian Church (1925), in *A Monograph of the Work of Warren, Knight & Davis Architects*, by the Architectural Catalog Company of New York.

National Influences

Two great American architectural firms were practitioners of the chief styles of church building in the early twentieth century. The New York firm of McKim, Mead, and White produced superb classical buildings, including a number of churches. Their most influential designer was Stanford White (1853-1906). Perhaps his greatest building was the domed, Corinthian Madison Square Presbyterian Church in New York, designed and built from 1904 to 1906. The Boston and New York firm of Cram, Goodhue, and Ferguson, whose theorist was Ralph Adams Cram (1863-1924) and chief designer Bertram Grosvenor Goodhue (1869-1924), developed a scholarly, inventive, and spacious Gothic style which inspired emulators all over the country.

William T. Warren (1877-1962) and William L. Welton (1874-1934) came to Birmingham in 1907 after they had completed their architectural training as draftsmen in the office of McKim, Mead, and White in the years before White's death in 1906. Both Warren and Welton would also have seen the designs by Goodhue for correctly Neo-Gothic St. Thomas Episcopal Church on Fifth Avenue in New York City. Its construction began in 1905 and was a reproving correction to the eclectic exuberance of Renwick's St. Patrick's just down the street. Work on St. Thomas continued as late as 1913 so that Eugene Knight (1884-1971), who came to Birmingham in 1902 and first worked for Charles Wheelock, then for William Weston, would have seen it rising during the two different years he lived and trained in New York in 1910 and 1913. Warren and Knight's Independent Presbyterian Church (1926) is an essay in Neo-Gothic of the kind Cram and Goodhue espoused.

Hugh Martin (1874-1959) was in New York (1894-1897), earlier than Warren, Welton, and Knight, when he worked for R. H. Robertson (1849-1919). It was during these years that Robertson designed the Renaissance St. Paul's Methodist Episcopal Church in New York (1897). Martin came to Birmingham in 1899, worked for Wheelock for a year, and, in 1900, joined John A. Miller in the partnership of Miller and Martin. Wallace Rayfield (1874-1941), who came to Birmingham in 1907, was an architectural student in New York from 1897 to 1899. He and Martin must both have been aware of the great complex of buildings rising on the new Columbia University campus, begun in 1893, many of them designed by McKim, Mead, and White. That firm also made designs for buildings for the World's Columbian Exposition of 1893 in Chicago. In that vast array of temporary classical structures the dream of an American Renaissance architecture found complete expression. The chief planner for the exposition was D. H. Burnham of Chicago (1846-1912). It was in Burnham's office that young William Weston (1866-1932) began his architectural training in 1885, and he may well still have been there in 1892. Weston came to Birmingham in 1902 and left in 1915. Knight completed his office training with Weston, and, Knight, in practice by himself after Weston's departure, gave young George Turner his first office training from 1915 to 1917, before Turner began his architectural education at the University of Pennsylvania.

Old South Avondale Baptist Church (1914), architect J. E. Green.

Temple Beth-El (1926) architect: Charles McCauley.

Classical Style

The classical training of some Birmingham architects of the early twentieth century is evident in William Welton's Walker Memorial Methodist Church (1918), *below*, with a superb portico of doubled Ionic columns, and his Ruhama Baptist (1923), Tuscan hexastyle. Warren and Welton's unbuilt design for Southside Baptist Church (1909) is an enlargement of Renaissance forms beneath a great dome. Wallace Rayfield's Sixteenth Street Baptist Church (1909) has arched and pedimented side walls, consciously reflective of the ordered, balanced classicism of the American Renaissance. Weston (assisted by Knight) designed Temple Emanu-El (1911), a Corinthian columned and domed expression of the American Renaissance style.

New Community United Methodist Church-Old Walker Memorial Methodist Church (1918), architect: William L. Welton.

Nothing is known about the education or previous architectural experience of James E. Green, but two of his Birmingham churches exemplify the classicism of the American Renaissance. They are South Avondale Baptist (1914), Ionic and domed, and Calvary Baptist (1922), its interior grandly walled by giant engaged Corinthian pilasters with gilded capitals. Southside Baptist, as designed by R. H. Hunt of Chattanooga (1862-1937) and built in 1910 and 1911, is a Roman Ionic temple, a late example of Classical Revival architecture.

Colonial Revival Styles

There are two kinds of Colonial Revival churches in Birmingham. Both are developments of the work done by major national figures. The American Colonial Revival, which is classical and the continuation of the architecture of the English colonies on the Atlantic seaboard before the Revolution, recollects and exalts the pre-revolutionary Anglo-American past. It is a special and simpler outgrowth of the American Renaissance triumph expressed by the World's Columbian Exposition of 1893. One important national architect of Colonial churches was Ralph Adams Cram in his various partnerships. The Cram firm designed churches like the Phillips Church in Exeter, New Hampshire (1896-1899). It also built a whole Colonial Revival college campus for Sweet Briar College in Virginia (1905-1907). Two Birmingham Colonial Revival churches are the third Hunter Street Baptist Church (1956-1958) designed by George Turner, and Canterbury United Methodist Church, Mountain Brook (1961), designed by Frederick W. Renneker (1908-1991), *page 4*. In 1931, Canterbury had considered a Gothic design by the Birmingham firm of Denham and Denham. Charles H. McCauley (1893-1970) proposed a Colonial design for the church before the adoption of Renneker's. The forms of Renneker's interior engaged Corinthian pilasters are simpler and less boldly projecting than James Green's pilasters in Calvary Baptist. Renneker had his architectural training at Auburn University and his first office experience with Miller and Martin in Birmingham, a firm which did much Colonial work. Hunter Street Baptist has more delicate internal column forms, but the aisles they form break up the immense interior space. The exterior stone pilasters engaged in the brick walls form a sober frame for the extravagent broken pediment over the main entrance door. It is another Birmingham architectural firm, Davis, Speake which gave Birmingham the design for Samford University, a classical American Colonial college campus with a fine Colonial chapel.

The other kind of Colonial Revival church is Spanish Colonial Revival. A very early example of this is

Highlands Methodist Church of 1907 by the Atlanta architect P. Thornton Marye (1872-1935). The details of its forms are the twisted, multiply curved yet broken forms of the Spanish Churrigueresque style of the eighteenth century and its Spanish American adaptions. The textbook national example of this style is a little later, Bertram Goodhue's tower at the Panama California Exposition of 1911 to 1915 in San Diego. There is much Spanish Revival architecture in Birmingham, especially in Homewood. It is, of course, a recollection of the non-English Colonial past of Florida and California. George Turner did a fine small Spanish Revival building for Central Park Presbyterian Church in 1926. This was doubled in size by Van Keuren, Davis & Co. in 1948. The enlargement is a sensitive expansion. Arched windows, stucco walls, the red tile roof, and the two-stage tower with polygonal belfry all express the Spanish Revival. The play of arch and patterned decoration which is Spanish (and also a little Moorish) appears also in the façade of Temple Beth-El on Highland Avenue, designed by Charles McCauley in 1926, *page 6*.

Liturgical Influences

The form of the churches of Birmingham is a function of their theological teaching and liturgical style. Each Birmingham church answers the question, "What is a church for?" Liturgy — the practice of worship and the doing of it — shapes plan and space, and these change as liturgical practice changes.

Theological concept and liturgical form continue and express medieval and sixteenth-century Reformation perceptions of the church building and formulations of its architecture. These perceptions underwent further transformation during the seventeenth-century Counter Reformation, the reaction of the nineteenth-century Oxford Movement in England, the response of twentieth-century Protestantism to the liturgical and architectural reforms of the Oxford Movement, and, finally, the transforming thinking about the setting for Christian worship which underlies the ecumenical reform of Christian worship in the second half of the twentieth century.

By the thirteenth century, the period of the earlier Gothic architecture, the medieval Catholic doctrine about the church building was well established. The church is God's house; it is heaven's gate; so it is to be dedicated and consecrated as a holy place altogether belonging to God. Its sacred character makes it an image of heaven, and so men must make it glorious, exalted, and mighty and strong. The great Gothic churches express these qualities in their height, arches, vaults, jewel-colored light, and exalted towers. Every continuation and revival of Gothic subscribe to this concept of the church as God's holy place.

Interior, Avondale United Methodist Church (1931), architect: Miller and Martin.

At the Reformation, this Gothic notion of the church building received qualified Anglican approval, radical Calvinist correction, and intermediate Lutheran amendment. For the Anglican Richard Hooker, "the house of prayer is a Court beautified with the presence of celestial powers; [so] that there we stand, we pray, we sound forth hymns unto God, having His Angels intermingled as our associates." (*Laws of Ecclesiastical Polity* [1597], V, 25, 2)

French theologian John Calvin disagrees: "there is need of great caution, lest we consider them [churches] as the proper habitations of the Deity, where he may be nearer to us to hear our prayers—an idea which has begun to be prevalent for several ages—or ascribe to them I know not what mysterious sanctity, which might be supposed to render our devotions more holy in the Divine view." (*Institutes of the Christian Religion* [1536], III, 20, 30) German reformer Martin Luther's position is intermediate: "this new house . . . may be rightly and Christianly consecrated and blessed, not like the papists' churches with their bishop's chrism and censing, but according to God's command and will, [and so] we shall begin by hearing and expounding God's Word, and then . . . call upon him together and say the Lord's prayer." (*Sermon for the Consecration of Torgau [Castle] Chapel*, 1544)

The churches of Birmingham, then, are theologically of at least three kinds. Some are fortresses of God enshrining the altar throne of his holy mystery adored by angels and men. The focal point is a distant altar,

St. George Melkite Church (1959), architect: Van Keuren, Davis & Co.

often with sacred images set behind or around it. Stained glass is figurative and often teaches doctrine. St. Paul's, Advent, St. Mary's, Blessed Sacrament, Holy Trinity-Holy Cross, and St. George express this belief. Other churches follow Calvin in the severity of their comparative plainness. Such is South Avondale Baptist, at least inside, but there are few surviving churches in Birmingham which are merely preaching barns. Those more like what Luther speaks of are the numerous Protestant churches which are Word-centered churches designed for the reading of scripture, preaching and prayer. First Methodist, Ensley Baptist, East Lake Methodist, and Sixteenth Street Baptist are churches of this kind. They are great auditoriums: balconied and approaching squareness in plan. Their focus is the central place for the reading and preaching of

St. Luke's Episcopal Church, Mountain Brook (1961), architect: Nelson Smith.

scripture. People spread wide before the preacher, even surround and are above him, always immediately before him, gathered with him in the community of prayer.

The Oxford Movement

In the nineteenth century in England, the Oxford Movement in the Church of England was a revival of medieval liturgical practice and also of Gothic style in church building. The model for the architectural and liturgical revival was not, however, that of the ordinary local church. Instead, it was that of the great cathedral churches. They were richly and elaborately decorated and had complex and multiple part interiors. The suggestion of transepts and the comparatively deep chancel at Advent, the cross plan and projecting chancel at St. Mary's, even, much later, the aisles set off from the nave by piers and side chapels of St. Luke's in Mountain Brook (1961) are Oxford Movement corrections of post medieval church planning in England. The Oxford Movement was influential in the Episcopal Church in the United States, but in the long run it altered the church interiors of mainline Protestantism. Both First Presbyterian and South Highland Presbyterian were planned as Word-centered churches (churches in which the hearing and contemplating the "word of God" is the primary activity). Both were converted from focus on a central pulpit in an essentially rectangular space to a longer room focused upon a raised altar with a central aisle leading to it and a pulpit to one side of this central axis. The change happened at First Presbyterian in 1921. The architects were Warren, Knight & Davis. They were the designers of Independent Presbyterian Church which had length, a central aisle, an axial altar, and complex Gothic space in its 1926 building. Canterbury Methodist Church, which had planned an English Perpendicular Gothic structure in 1931, has a Georgian rather than a Gothic style in its building of 1961, but its plan is Gothic. There is a central aisle, a deep chancel, a central altar, and even a divided choir.

Funding and Support

This essay has dealt with the necessity for churches, their styles, the interrelated careers of their architects, and their theological purposes. Anyone who has ever been involved in building a church knows that money is fundamental and that money comes from givers, and giving is moved, attracted, and shaped by leadership. The story of this leadership is complicated for every church. Many good church histories rehearse leaders' particular accomplishments, the tale of how they did it, once, twice, three times, even four. How much did it cost to build a church in Birmingham in the century this book covers? We have information for 20 of the 37 buildings illustrated in this book. Sometimes we know the proposed cost and the actual cost. Cost is probably nearly always for the building only, not furnishings, organ, and other equipment. Cost probably does not include the architect's fee.

First Presbyterian was supposed to cost $25,000 and did cost $33,500 in 1886 to 1888. Advent as designed in 1890 in richly ornamented stone was to cost $65,000. As built, unornamented and minimally finished inside, it cost $40,000. The Presbyterians used brick with terra cotta ornament and metal interiors. The Episcopalians built in stone with carved ornament and large timber framing to support the wide roof. St. Mary's bought its lot for $3,250, and built its stone church with wood framed roof for $23,250 in 1891 to 1892. This seems modest, but the roof spans are narrower and the framing made from smaller members than at Advent. The Cathedral of St. Paul cost about $90,000 from 1890 to 1893. It is brick and wood with some stone and is more complex and ornamented than Advent or St. Mary's. The extravagant building of the 1880s and 1890s was First Methodist in Birmingham, and the litany of its increasing costs must have been daunting to those who had to pay them. In August 1890, it was to cost $80,000, in September, $100,000, in January 1891, $125,000, in June $150,000, and the final cost grew to $160,000. The brick Methodist church of 1882 had cost only $20,000. The cost did not include the land, which was the gift of Col. James W. Sloss. Thomas T. Hillman gave $30,000 of the cash amount expended. Special costs, perhaps included in this large figure, are: frescoing for $2,000; the central chandelier for $4,000; and the organ for $10,000. The high cost of First Methodist does include much education space, a major tower, and massive stone construction. South Highland Presbyterian was less costly in 1892, only about $25,000, which was inexpensive for this stone building.

In the early twentieth century, Sixteenth Street Baptist cost $62,000 in 1911 and Southside Baptist $75,000 in the same year. Southside Baptist was built in brick and stone, but this is much more than the $50,000 their brick church of 1892 had cost them. The church history notes that the cost of the 1911 building with fixtures and organ rose to $87,000. Highlands Methodist cost about $100,000 in 1907 to 1909. This expenditure did not finish the tower of this elaborate building. The land had been acquired in 1904 for about $15,000. Woodlawn Methodist was finished in 1912, in stone and with some education space in the basement level. It cost $65,000. South Avondale Baptist was completed in 1916 for $30,000. This brick and wood building took two years to build because of delays when work stopped because there was no money in hand.

Sardis Baptist Church-Old Hunter Street Baptist (1927), architect: N. O. Patterson.

Costs rise after World War I. Ruhama Baptist spent $150,000 for the auditorium only. The education building was completed first. Even the modest education and church building of Trinity Methodist in Homewood cost $31,800 in 1928. This was stone and with elaborate carved stone details. Two large buildings of the 1920s were most expensive. The architects calculated that the construction costs for the sanctuary only of Independent Presbyterian Church were $171,112. This figure included neither furnishings nor the architect's fee. Independent Presbyterian is an elaborate Gothic building in stone, much of it complexly carved, but this cost did not include stained glass or the organ. Ensley Baptist Church was estimated to have cost $250,000 when the auditorium was

Chapel, South Highland Presbyterian Church (1953), architect: Van Keuren, Davis & Co.

Sixth Avenue Baptist Church (1967), architect: Lawrence Whitten.

finished in 1929. This may have included the education building, the organ and furnishings. The building is brick, Gothic, elaborate, and very large. Like many churches in the 1920s, Ensley Baptist borrowed to finish construction. Their loan was $175,000, which they had trouble paying during the Great Depression. The final payment was made in 1946. This heavy debt burden and slow payment was typical for many churches.

Macedonia Missionary Baptist Church, Ensley (1965), architect: Lawrence Whitten.

After World War II

After the Great Depression and World War II, church building resumed with vigor and at new levels of expenditure. Holy Trinity-Holy Cross Cathedral, brick with some stone trim, was built for $225,000 in 1949 and 1950. Highlands Methodist, which had spent $100,000 to build from 1907 to 1909, spent $350,000 in 1949 to reverse the interior of the church, add a new divided chancel and axial altar, and build a balcony. A few years later, Hunter Street Baptist spent $450,000 to build its new Colonial brick and limestone sanctuary. In 1959 St. George Church paid $254,000 to build its new brick and concrete building, not particularly large. From 1961 to 1962, St. Luke's built its concrete and brick building for $550,000. The new organ cost only $6,500. In the same years, Canterbury Methodist built its immense new sanctuary at a cost of $950,000, page 3.

Given the cost of church building at any time, it is not surprising that many churches are simply done. Yet simplicity can be varied and even richly complex. In the last thirty years, historians and critics of architecture have come to have an increasing respect for architecture designed by amateurs or less sophisticated practitioners. This is now called "vernacular architecture." Two Birmingham churches illustrate vernacular design of high quality. St. Joseph's Catholic Church in Ensley (1914) has some Classicial features on its simple exterior. Inside is a spectacular oak frame that imposes the separation of nave and aisles within a pitched-roofed space. The arched beams are semicircular, un-Gothic, but in the angle between the vertical posts and the transverse beams meeting the Corinthian capitals on the posts there are set cusped, Gothic roundels. The unknown architect chooses to have the best of both of the dominant architectural languages of his time.

The second vernacular building is the second Hunter Street Baptist (1927) by the Baptist minister-architect N. O. Patterson. Its semicircular arched porch and windows, Palladian window in the pedimental gable, and elaborate classical cornices are clearly related to American Renaissance architectural forms, but the short projecting towers and high basement are unsophisticated customary arrangements as important as the stylistic references. Patterson was concerned with cost. He made his pastoral ministry an architectural ministry, in part to keep down building costs, page 9.

The post World War II building boom for housing and for suburban expansion drew churches in its wake. The Birmingham newspapers have an astonished article about new church building nearly every year in the 1950s and early 1960s. Aspirations continue. It is in this time that new styles appear in church buildings. Many buildings are traditional, like the Colonial style of Canterbury Methodist or the fine, scholarly Gothic of the new chapel for South Highland Presbyterian Church added in 1953 and 1954 by Van Keuren, Davis & Co., *page 9.* Yet the same firm designs the most modern of Birmingham churches: St. George Melkite Catholic Church (1959), *page 8.* Despite some internal references to the Byzantine past, St. George is a spare, taut, clever exercise in the International Style which dominates its immediate neighborhood.

More cautious and traditional is Macedonia Missionary Baptist Church built in 1965 in Ensley. Lawrence Whitten (1906-1968) did a number of churches of this kind, some more radical than Macedonia, *page 10.* All of the language of the Colonial still appears, but it is flattened, simplified, used referentially rather than descriptively, and so a modernizing transformation appears.

Nelson Smith (1910-1997) sought to achieve a radical new structural and contemporary form in his design for St. Luke's in Mountain Brook. Resistance to his vision resulted in a compromise of modern concrete material and catenary arches with the traditional division into nave and aisles, rectangular space, and even Colonial Revival windows, *page 8.* Lawrence Whitten designed Woodlawn Baptist and Central Park Baptist, both less traditional than the Ensley church. He also designed Sixth Avenue Baptist in its late 1960s location on Martin Luther King, Jr. Drive, *page 10.* The simple cubic forms collect their compelling masses around the strong central punctuation of the tower. There is nothing historicist or banal about this design.

Lawrence Whitten, trained at Auburn, was white. Wallace A. Rayfield, architect of the Sixteenth Street

Three Ministers in Prayer, (1992), Kelly Ingram Park, in front of Sixteenth Street Baptist Church, Raymond Kaskey.

Baptist Church, was black. These two Birmingham architects each built in the forefront of the architectural style of his day to meet the faithful aspirations of their clients. They sought to give architectural form to the place of preaching and of prayer. Like Philip Mewhinney for the Baptists in Ensley or George Kramer for the Methodists in Birmingham, they gave prayer its gathering room. And like the ministers at prayer in Raymond Kaskey's monument in Kelly Ingram Park, they looked upon holiness. To contain and express the glory of holiness is the art of St. George and the chapel of South Highlands. They are linked in this achievement to the vision in Wheelock's Advent, Druiding's St. Paul's, and Turner's East Lake Methodist. That vision is Jacob's, to set up what shall show that "Surely the Lord is in this place, . . . this is none other but the house of God, and this is the gate of heaven." (Genesis 28:16-17)

Cathedral Church of the Advent (Episcopal)

Twentieth Street at Sixth Avenue North
Built: 1887-1893, 1895
Charles Wheelock & Son

When the Church of the Advent was finished in 1893, the houses of prosperous Birmingham, still a young city, surrounded it. The towers of The Cathedral of St. Paul, First Presbyterian, and First Methodist stood above the rooftops, and the people of Advent found the money to complete their tower in 1895, in spite of the financial depression of the early 1890s.

Today the church has become a cathedral and a skyscraper rises beside it and another across the street. Seen from the AmSouth/Harbert plaza across Birmingham Green, *left*, this wide, bold, sturdy, densely rusticated building is the economically necessary simplification of the late Victorian Gothic design for the church published in the *Birmingham Age Herald* on 13 October 1889. This design has two towers, immense traceried windows, tall finials on the corners of the towers and on every buttress, and gables over every arch. The church as built simplifies, condenses and focuses the published design to a freely eclectic, grandly wide-spreading, Neo-Romanesque mass. Only the pointed arches of the porch and windows and the finials on the tower still suggest the Gothic style. The foundations laid in 1887 determine the width of the broad plan.

Charles Wheelock (1833-1910), the architect of Advent and a member of the church, had come to Birmingham to practice architecture in 1881. His son, Harry B. Wheelock (1866-1940), had just become his partner in 1887. The design of the façade plays with arched vertical openings, horizontal bands, and variously roughened surfaces. Horizontal bands of masonry tie the arches of the windows together at the base of their springing. These horizontals are repeated above the triple arch of the porch, twice across the pointed windows, and below and above the topmost row of windows. The rustication of the masonry changes too. In the lower parts of the front wall, the blocks are of irregular size, their projection restrained, and their joints not deeply marked. The central gable changes above the topmost horizontal to become a geometric pattern of projecting bosses. The tower stage of 1895 changes again, the blocks become larger, the rustication bolder, the joints deeper. Wheelock's imagination at the Advent suggests some of the variation of forms and surfaces in the *Alabama Moon* sculpture by Clyde Lynds in the AmSouth/Harbert plaza and in the AmSouth/Harbert tower itself.

The weighty and densely carved cushion capitals of the Advent porch, *above,* are medievalized Corinthian with volutes and rosette patera. The doors leading from the porch into the church were designed by Arthur Geissler of New York after 1926. Thus, they are far more correctly Gothic than the church for which they provide the entrance.

The wide nave of Advent, *right,* is covered by a hammerbeam roof. The hammerbeams terminate in classical volutes. From the hammerbeams spring the wooden arches that carry the breadth of the wide roof. The structural stability of the span is assured by the nineteenth-century expedient of metal tie rods. The three arches that terminate the nave cleverly suggest spaces more vast and deep than exist. Stained glass windows on either side of the altar were installed in 1898; the altar and reredos four years later in 1902.

Advent is a city church, set close to its street corner. The sturdy mass of the tower marks the intersection. The lowest tower window was walled up to form the background for the 1965 bronze copy of the marble Christ (1821) by the Danish sculptor Bertel Thorvaldsen. The forceful breadth and strong tower of the building prevail against the impersonal anonymity of its skyscraper neighbor (the Financial Center, to the right in the photograph) and partly suggest the colors, masses and surface variety of the AmSouth/Harbert tower across Twentieth Street.

The breadth of the nave of Advent makes it a preaching church, and the towering authority of this pulpit also makes that evident. The chancel furnishings and organ screens are later enrichments of the interior, replacing earlier, simpler, and less correctly Gothic work. The pulpit and its canopy, probably carved in Germany and installed about 1905, are the outstanding pieces of furnishing. The trumpeting angels atop the canopy celebrate preaching, and the figures of Jesus and the four evangelists carved on the faces of the pulpit itself also proclaim the word of God.

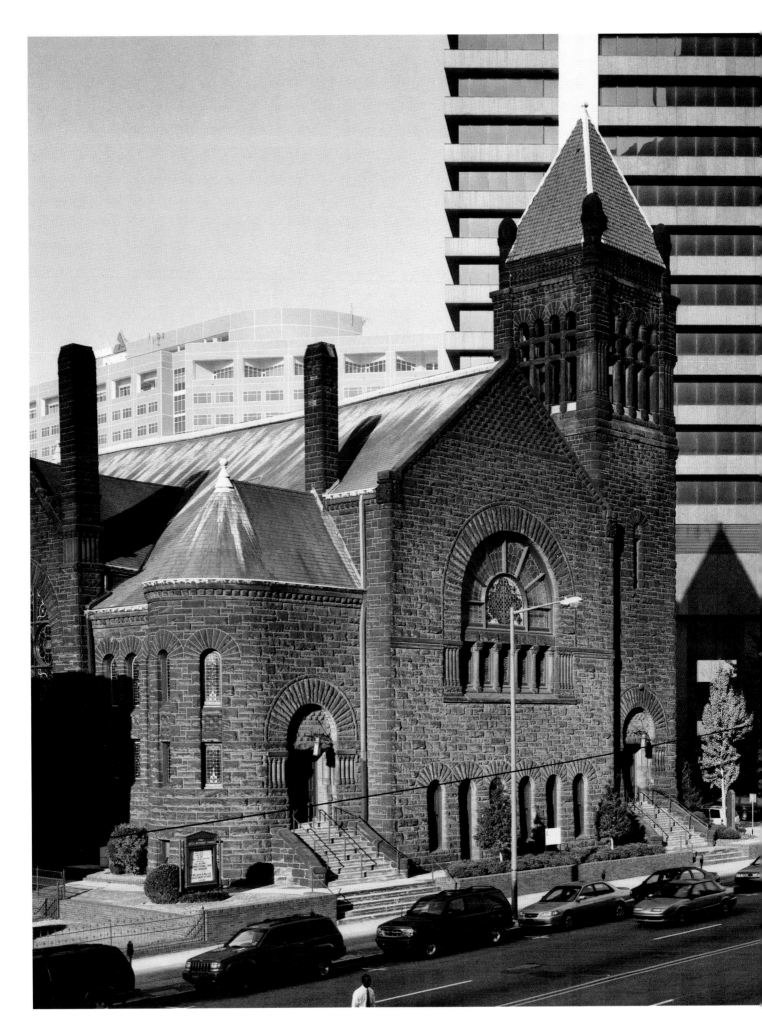

First United Methodist Church of Birmingham

Nineteenth Street at Sixth Avenue North
Built: September 1890-December 1891
Architect: Weary and Kramer, Akron, Ohio

First United Methodist Church is the third church built by this congregation in the first eighteen years of its life. It is a superb design in the American Romanesque style invented by the architect H. H. Richardson for Trinity Church, Boston, finished as recently as 1877. George W. Kramer (1847-1938), the design partner of Weary and Kramer, published the Birmingham building in his 1897 book, *The What, Why, and How of Church Building*. The Birmingham church is more somber and simple than its Boston model, but it echoes the bold sweep of curving walls and the weighty roughness of the immense stones in the arches. This is a modern American church building of the sort still new in the 1890s. The whole basement level is devoted to space for church programs, then a relatively new idea in church building.

This and other downtown churches, when they were new, stood in neighborhoods of large houses, densely set around them. Their towers marked their presence and signaled the place of entrance. Worshipers at First Methodist ascended the flights of steps from Nineteenth Street to enter the corners of the sanctuary on either side of the pulpit, in the face of the congregation. The present entrance to the building from Sixth Avenue passes through an immense vestibule formed from the original great semicircle of the Sunday School Room, which could seat a thousand people. The remodeling creating this entrance was done in 1973.

The interior of the First Methodist sanctuary remains one of the largest auditoriums in Birmingham, said, when it was built, to seat 2,400 persons. Congregation and choir are architecturally gathered at the gallery and main floor levels. The gallery flows into the choir loft, which is only a little lower. A little lower still and just above the railed holy table, the seats for the presiding clergy are in the midst of the congregation. The great circles of the stained glass windows in each side wall emphasize the circular effect of this square room. The ceiling lifts an unexpected central coved roof octagon, a final conclusion of the play between square and circle in this space.

First Methodist is an expensive building. As first envisioned, it was to cost $80,000. When finally completed, the cost had risen to $160,000.

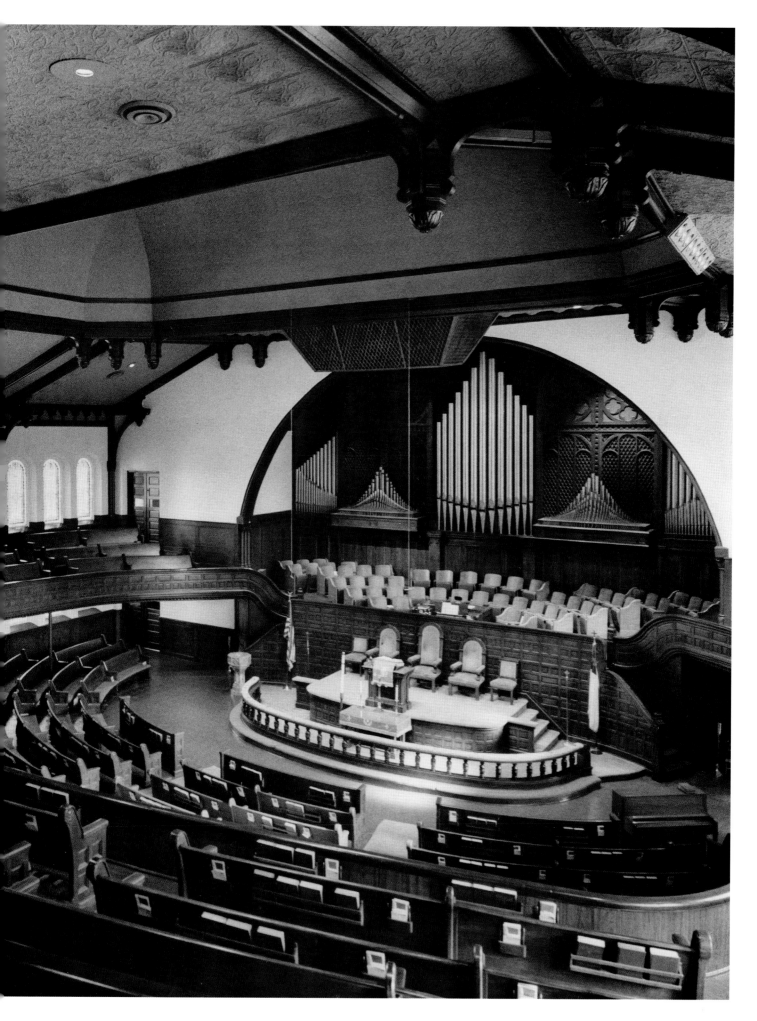

An entrance doorway in the Nineteenth Street facade of First Methodist, *left*, stresses the Romanesque cubic magnitude of the stonework. The single stone of the lintel of the door is nearly eight feet wide and nearly two feet deep and high. Its roughness contrasts with the smooth architraves over the flanking columns. The diaper work in the tympanum in the arch of the door also contrasts rough with smooth stone. The mighty stones of the door arch are the breadth of the four jamb columns.

The long side of the building, *above*, shows the stretch of its depth: tower narrow but tall, transept wider and tall, heightened by the chimneys that clasp its flanks. The education wing, *far right*, is wider still, two-storied, and multi-windowed. The light-catching, rich fretting of the various rusticated surfaces of this long facade energizes the sobriety of its grandeur.

First Presbyterian Church

Fourth Avenue North at Twenty-first Street
Built: 1886-1888
Architect: unknown

First Presbyterian Church is the oldest surviving church building in downtown Birmingham. The historian of the church writes that the building was executed "following the design of a noted church architect of New York." New York architects such as J. Wrey Mould (1825-1886) and Carl Pfeiffer (1834-1888) are possible designers. The church has the brilliant chromaticism of the best Victorian Gothic style of the 1870s and 1880s. This shows in the contrasting lozenges and flowers laid in the slating of the roof and the contrast of red-orange terracotta inlays with the deeper, more intense red of the brick walls. Surfaces and edges angle, facet, and curve. The facade is three-sided. The pinnacles on the façade and tower turrets have roofs with curving arrises. Alternate broad bands of roof slate have three-sided ends for each slate.

The entrance on Fourth Avenue replaced a taller window with a new door and smaller window above. This remodeling of 1921 by the Birmingham architectural firm of Warren and Knight, was made necessary by the widening of Twenty-first Street, which blocked easy access to the original door from Twenty-first.

The First Presbyterian interior is seen from the 1921 entrance, as rearranged then, and facing the 1950 remodeling which placed the choir in the organ gallery and opened a new rose window above it. These changes do not alter the character of the extraordinary and intimate iron room designed from 1886 to 1888. Cylindrical iron posts carry rusticated iron basket capitals which support a fragmentary classical entablature of iron. From the capitals rise the pointed cross of arched surfaces. These are stone form-shapes made of iron imitating medieval wooden imitations of stone. The original entrance opened through the tower set in the near left corner of this square cross. The pulpit was originally placed in the transept to the right. The room makes a low and intimate contrast to the high pitch of the external roofs and the tall spire with corner pinnacles flanking steep gables above the large belfry openings divided by Gothic tracery.

The Cathedral of St. Paul

Third Avenue North at Twenty-second Street
Built: 1890-1893
Architect: The Druiding Company, Chicago.

This Germanic style brick Gothic building was built as the parish church of the growing Catholic population of Birmingham. It became a cathedral with the creation of the Catholic diocese of Birmingham in 1969. St. Paul's is a late and spectacular design by the German-born, Midwestern architect Adolphus Druiding (1839-1899), a design characteristic of his work. The only major external change in the appearance of the building is the 1972 replacement of the great stained glass window over the entrance door by faceted glass set in concrete.

Druiding's design for St. Paul's is an eclectic combination of such essentially French Rayonnant elements as the clerestory windows beneath gables projecting from the roof of the nave and the spire-crowned twin towers, 185-feet-tall, which echo the facade of Cologne Cathedral, just being completed in the nineteenth century. The strong lines of white stone against red brick are less subtle than the work at First Presbyterian, but they are boldly and memorably assertive.

The sculpture of St. Paul's is one of three on the facade of the building which were once part of the sculptures related to the altars inside. These altars were remodeled and simplified from 1972 to 1973. The sculptures date from 1905.

This photograph of the interior of St. Paul's shows the view of the east aisle as it extends from the choir gallery to the apse. The aisle is narrow, tall, and vaulted with multiple, pointed Gothic arches. It ends in a polygonal apse, another Gothic feature. Two angels from the original main altar of 1905 now kneel in adoration on either side of the tabernacle in which the consecrated hosts (the bread of the communion) are kept.

The octagonal capitals, carved with several rows of deeply carved, stiffly geometric, square, leafy, Gothic forms are a soft, multi-surfaced contrast to the smooth, hard sheen of the granite shafts of the columns that separate the aisle from the nave.

Through the first arch of the arcade, one can see the 1905 altar that is 17 feet wide. The 1972 to 1973 renovations removed the original 25 foot superstructure that stood behind it, opening the space of the main apse. The cathedra or bishop's chair now sits in the center of this space. These architectural changes permit the liturgical practices directed by the Second Vatican Council of 1962 to 1965.

This view of St. Paul's shows what Gothic space is like. It is space multiple in breadth and height and distance. Its divisions are skeletal. Its outside walls are window-filled and walls and windows are bright with many colors.

The north end of the west wall of the nave, *left*, shows the aisle arcade and clerestory windows above it. Above the engaged wall shafts, the ribs of the nave vault spring. Colored patterns adorn the walls. Between the clerestory windows, colored paint imitates drafted stonework. The view of the nave, *above*, shows the tall aisles of the nave. The net of Gothic ribs in the apse vault is a dramatic conclusion to the linear complexity of the Gothic style church.

Sixteenth Street
Baptist Church

Sixth Avenue North at Sixteenth Street
Built: 1909-1911
Architect: W. A. Rayfield & Co.

A statue of Martin Luther King, Jr., beholds the
Sixteenth Street Baptist Church which has become
the Birmingham architectural icon of the courage,
cost, and power of the civil rights struggle of the
1950s and 1960s. When the church was built, it was
at a center of a prosperous black neighborhood that
was rising around what is now called Kelly Ingram
Park. The church stands at the edge of this park.
Wallace A. Rayfield (1872-1941), the architect of
the church, had taken a two-year architectural
diploma program at Pratt Institute in New York.
From New York he moved to Tuskegee Institute to
teach drafting. He stayed there until 1907, when he
set up his practice in Birmingham. Rayfield designed
more than 479 buildings, of which Sixteenth Street
Baptist Church is one of the most important. It
shows the training and skill of this successful black
architect in mid-career.

The design for the Sixteenth Street church is eclectic. There is Romanesque arcading for the entrance porch and tower openings, but the architectural language of the gable above the window over the porch, the central wooden lantern, and, above all, the elevation of the side wall show Rayfield's acquaintance with and mastery of the Beaux-Arts Classicism of the American Renaissance of ca. 1890 to 1910. The side wall has an academic palatial dignity, ultimately inspired by the classical exhibition halls of the World's Columbian Exposition of 1893 in Chicago.

Highlands United Methodist Church

Twentieth Street South at Five Points Circle
Built: 1907-1909, 1921, 1949-1952
Architect: P. Thornton Marye, Atlanta

The façade of Highlands United Methodist Church still dominates the Five Points Circle of the early suburban town of Highland. It is an early example of Spanish Colonial Revival architecture, built before the Panama-California Exhibition which popularized the style. The striking use of architectural terra-cotta in the broken pediments, urns, and ultimately in the details of the tower (not finished until 1921, under the design supervision of the architect Bem Price) shows the deft hand of P. Thornton Marye (1872-1935). Marye designed the Birmingham Terminal Station, before he designed the church. The station was grander, more sober and serious. Highlands is joyfully exuberant.

The pulpit originally stood between the two entrance doors of the façade, *right*, but the orientation of the interior was reversed from 1949 to 1952 when a new chancel was built by the architectural firm of Miller, Martin, and Lewis. The awkward box of masonry above and behind the right entrance door and the interior balcony over the entrances, *left*, are the result of this change.

The interior is more serious than the exterior. The side wall pictured shows the same Beaux-Arts Classicism that Wallace Rayfield was to use on the side wall of Sixteenth Street Baptist Church begun in 1909. While Highlands is more opulent, the language of controlled Classicism is the same. The Highlands Methodist interior is a contrast to the wild vigor of its Churrigueresque façade and tower belfry.

South Highlands United Methodist Church still dominates the Five Points Circle, *above*. But change came to the circle in the early twentieth century as commercial and apartment buildings joined early houses at this busy streetcar intersection. The high-rise Terrace Court Apartments were constructed a block up on Twentieth Street and the Dulion and La Salle apartments, *right*, rose behind South Highlands. By the 1930s, Art Deco commercial buildings, like the one on the left, walled the circle. The riotous vigor of Marye's ornament for the church façade and tower, *pictured right*, gives South Highlands the focus which masters these contending distractions.

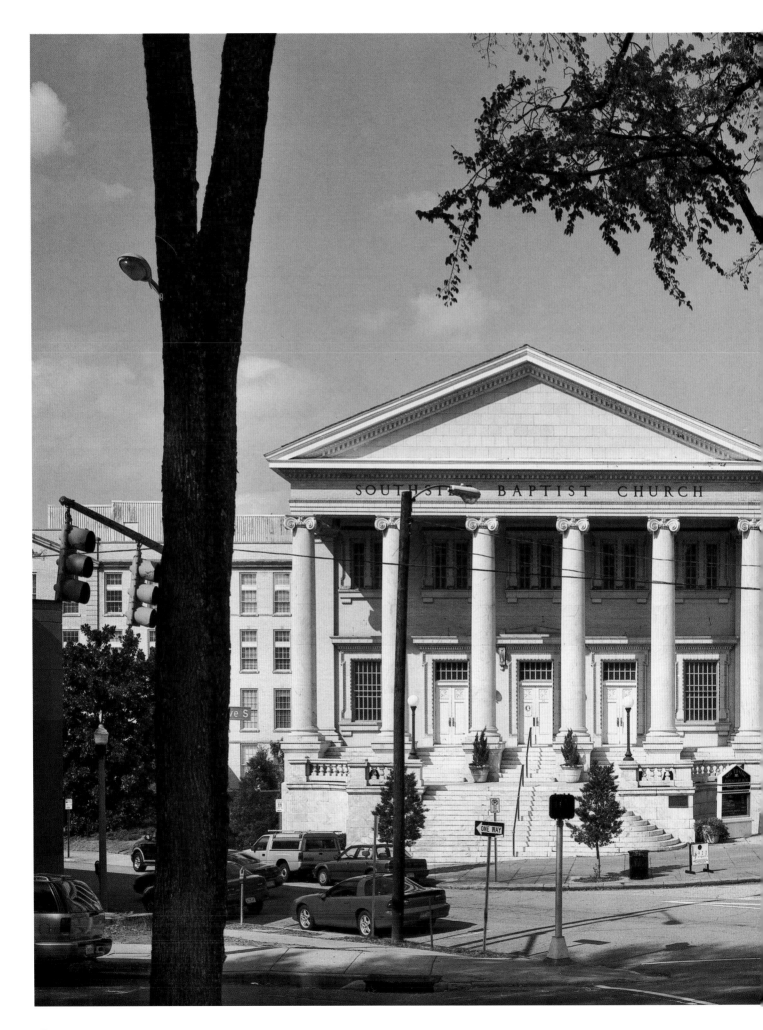

Southside Baptist Church

Eleventh Avenue South at Nineteenth Street
Built: 1910-1911
Architect: Reuben Harrison Hunt, Chattanooga

This sober Roman Ionic temple was built within sight of the just completed Highlands Methodist Church. Southside Baptist Church is a far more conservative design than the immense domed and towered building which the young architects, Warren and Welton, originally had proposed to the Baptists but which the church decided not to build. Reuben Harrison Hunt (1862-1937) designed this church and two others in the Birmingham area, the now destroyed First Baptist Church in downtown Birmingham (1902), and the First United Methodist Church of Bessemer (1914).

What is unexpected about Southside Baptist are the curving forms of the entrance stairs and the incurvate elaboration of the balustraded terrace in front of the church. Perhaps the thrusting projection of the terrace prepares for the emphasis of the projecting entrance door frames, especially the central one carried on pronounced tall consoles and with a cornice more Corinthian than Ionic.

43

St. Mary's-on-the-Highlands Episcopal Church

Twelfth Avenue South at Nineteenth Street
Built: 1891-1892
Architect: John Sutcliffe

The present St. Mary's-on-the-Highlands building is the rapidly built $23,500 replacement of the church's burned wooden predecessor which stood on the Five Points Circle. The new church, like the old one, has a tower in the angle of intersecting nave and transepts. This arrangement compares with the then recently completed First Presbyterian Church, but St. Mary's is a two-story building with a raised basement for social and educational purposes, like the First Methodist Church under construction at the same time.

Stylistically the exterior is eclectically medieval. The rusticated stonework and corbeled arcading on the tower are Richardsonian Romanesque. The pointed window arches and large expanses of glass and the interior openness are Gothic. The building towers at the edge of its steep slope, but it is not quite so heavy and solid as it now seems. The arched room to the left of the entrance was originally an open porch.

The St. Mary's interior is extraordinary. Most who visit it will be overcome by the surrounding blazing glory of the complete ensemble of Munich and Munich-style stained glass. The brightness obscures the structure of the astonishing roof which this photograph remarkably reveals. Two great wooden arches spring from short diagonal hammerbeams to span the central space and to brace and carry the central diagonal rafters which support the valleys of the cross-shaped steep roof. Other transverse arches from hammerbeams separate chancel, transepts, and short nave from the central space. This roof is a wonder of space and wooden engineering.

St. Mary's architect John Sutcliffe (1853-1913) was born near Manchester, England, trained by his father as an architect, and came to Birmingham at the end of 1886. Six years later, he moved to Chicago where he made a new and successful career. He designed more than a hundred churches after this remarkable beginning at St. Mary's.

Temple Emanu-El

Highland Avenue at Twenty-first Street South
Built: 1911-1913
Architect: William C. Weston

Much of what makes excellent architecture is attention to detail. The photographs of the richly modeled Corinthian portico, where the acanthus leaves are crisply frilled and each helix is a tight coil, *left*, and Roman Doric temple-front screen, *below*, enclosing the Ark for the Torah of Temple Emanu-El show an architectural assurance that is massive without and deft and subtle within. The architect who received the commission was William C. Weston (1866-1932). His firm was large by 1911, when he employed Eugene Knight, after Knight's return from New York. In New York Knight had worked for the nationally prominent firm of Clinton and Russell. Knight, who took over Weston's practice after 1914, later claimed to have designed Temple Emanu-El.

Gothic, Classic, Brutalist, the styles of the twentieth century, change and confront one another at Highland Avenue and Twenty-first Street, *above*. South Highland Presbyterian is seen, *left*, from the rear: many-roofed, towered, of multiple parts, and with its Gothic pointed arches. The office tower, on the right, is a hard, plain square of heavy concrete masses. This hardness and heaviness give it the look of the Brutalist style of the 1960s and 1970s. In between, is the domed block of Temple Emanu-El. Every element of its Corinthian order is assured, and its entablature continues around the whole building, binding together the rising unity of its masses.

The 72-foot-dome, *right*, curves down to the arches that convert the cubic exterior to an octagon. The dome appears to be made of stone, not of wood and canvas. It hovers gracefully over the generous and open space. In the front of the room, at the rear of the bema, the shrine of the Torah fills the arch beneath a column-framed projecting pavilion capped by a broken pediment. This central feature in the Roman Doric screen is, appropriately, the grandest interior design.

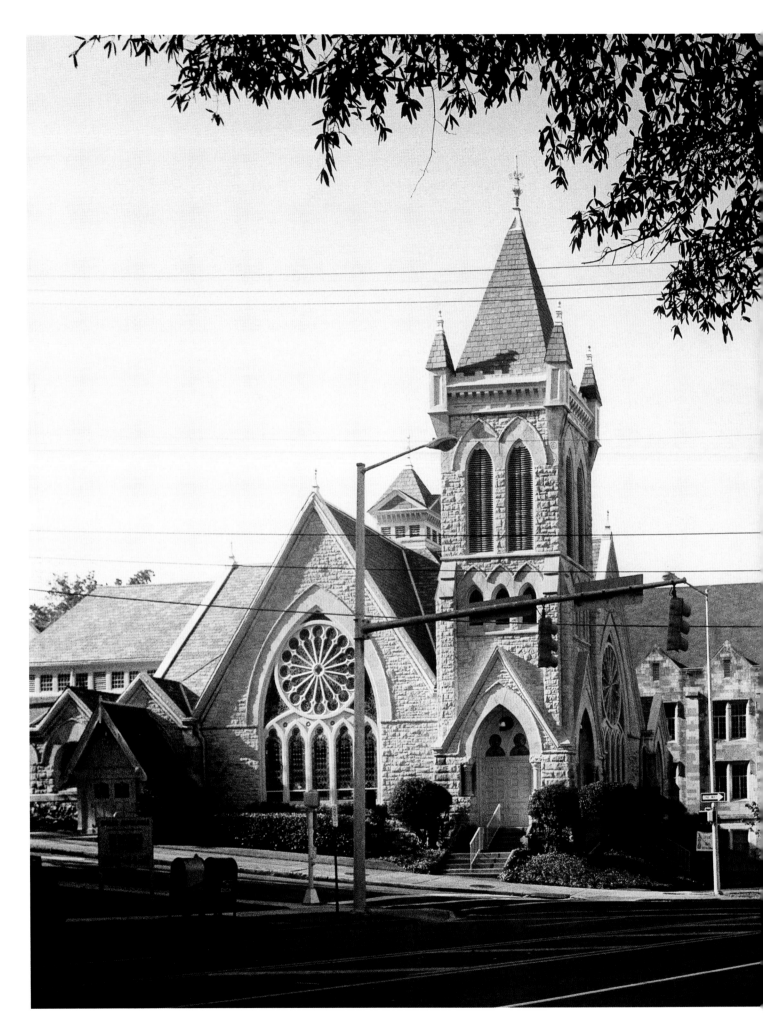

South Highland Presbyterian Church

Highland Avenue at Twenty-first Street South
Built: 1891-1892
Architect: Daniel Andrew Helmich

Daniel Andrew Helmich (1854-1917) was one of the two Birmingham architects whose practice survived the national financial panic and depression of the early 1890s. South Highland Presbyterian Church, a vigorous late Victorian, hard, heavy, rough Neo-Gothic structure, is Helmich's greatest work. The projecting rusticated moldings might have been conceived by H. H. Richardson. The space for worship has a Greek cross plan, emphasized in the double-hipped roof rising to a central ventilator lantern with a fantastic spiral finial.

In two windows to the left of the leftmost side entrance, *above*, the severity of the smooth stone arches contrasts sharply with the rustication of most of the masonry surface. The church extended its reach along Highland Avenue with the addition of the first Education Building (1925, William Welton, architect) and its further enlargement. The small chapel (1953-1954, E. B. Van Keuren and Charles F. Davis, Jr., architects) with its smooth gable front turns back toward the main sanctuary. Major additions made to the rear, uphill side (1998, Davis Architects) complement the earlier structure while solving present day accessibility problems.

South Highland's patterns of stone show clearly in this view of a window wall. This wall was originally behind the congregation. The adjacent tower along Twenty-first Street served as the principal entrance. The arches of the entrance door, the tower, and the window are smooth big blocks, widening as the arch rises to its point. The narrow course of stone that projects from the wall at the springing of the arch of the window is repeated in the rusticated projection of rough stone at the outer edge of each arch. The wooden tracery of the big window is boldly molded into freely inventive Gothic tracery which is a dark framing foil for the brilliant geometry of the stained glass as it is seen from the inside.

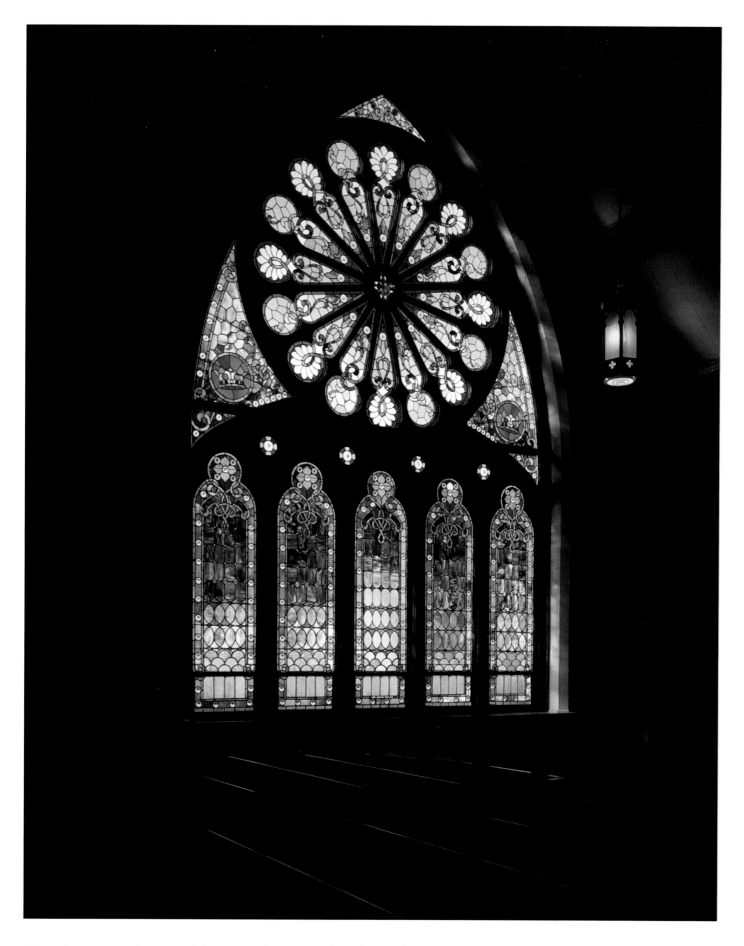

The ochre tint in the gray of the external stone work and the pink of the door jamb columns of South Highland's tower entrances are echoed in the brown and lavender hues of this stained glass window in South Highland, the work of an unknown designer. A similar huge window fills half the surface of the Highland Avenue street wall.

Stained Glass

Stained glass transfigures light to make it radiantly gem-like and so heavenly. To have stained glass was important. Probably more stained glass has been made in the United States since 1840 than was made in the whole of the Middle Ages from the twelfth to the sixteenth century. Most of the American glass was made for churches. Windows of standard designs could be bought from catalogues. Local stained glass craftsmen probably supplied standard designs, and might be asked to adjust or enlarge them to fit. There were also national and internationally known firms. Many of these did work in Birmingham. They include G. G. Riordan of Cincinnati at St. Paul's, the Franz Mayer Studios of Munich, Germany at Advent and St. Mary's-on-the-Highlands, the Jacoby Art Glass Studios of St. Louis at St. Mary's, and Nicola D'Ascenzo of Philadelphia, whose firm did the windows at Independent Presbyterian Church and also First Presbyterian. John Petts from Wales, designed a window for Sixteenth Street Baptist Church.

The windows at First United Methodist were in place when the church opened, and this was also achieved at Ruhama Baptist and Woodlawn Methodist. Other churches took many years to fill all their windows, as did the Cathedral of the Advent and Independent Presbyterian Church. At Independent, the work continued from 1938 to 1960.

• • • • •

The aisle windows of The Cathedral of St. Paul are the work of G. C. Riordan & Co. of Cincinnati. They were in place in 1893 when the church was first used. The three windows wholly visible through the granite columns that separate the aisle from the nave show, left to right, *St. Paul, St. John Berchman,* and *The Good Shepherd.* These figures are inserted panels within the decorative scheme used in all the windows. A rectangular panel at the base provides scrolls for a memorial inscription. The image is beneath a segmental arch which springs from flanking tabernacles of violet, yellow and turquoise blue. The cusped base of the arch is edged in pale green over a tympana of orange and a field of violet. The upper part of the arch is salmon and red-orange and a row of yellow trefoils crowns it. Suspended in front of it is a central tabernacle which turns its corner forward. Its chamber is blue, its gables filled with red fields. Above the segmental arch and behind the central tabernacle, small intersecting pointed yellow arches frame fields of flashing red. This upper arcade supports pale yellow Gothic finials upon a ground of lavender and blue-green. This palette of secondary hues is fin-de-siecle.

This corner view of the chancel of the Cathedral of the Advent centers on the 1898 window of the *Second Coming of Christ*, his new Advent. The maker is unknown, but the colors and forms are those of the new Art Nouveau style. The bright white-robed figure of Christ stands beneath a complex arched tabernacle with turret finial, rendered in gold and red. To the right is a window of the *Archangel Michael* and, to the left, the 1902 altar of the cathedral. The painting above it represents *The Last Supper*. It is a copy of a painting by the German painter Heinrich Von Hess.

The Advent's south transept window represents in the center the *Crucifixion*, and, on the sides, the *Resurrection, left,* and the *Ascension, right.* The windows were designed by the Franz Mayer Studios of Munich, Germany, makers of stained glass for churches all over the world. They were installed in 1902.

The stained glass of the First United Methodist Church downtown fills the two immense window walls that light the sanctuary with starry roundels set in a great cross. This glass fills the top of the window arch above the balcony. Below are four smaller windows, two of them figurative.

The windows were installed when the church was finished in 1891. As at St. Paul's, the dominant colors in the upper windows are yellow and violet with touches of red above. The dominant hue in the lower windows is green.

The windows of Woodlawn United Methodist Church (built 1909-1912) were installed in 1911. The glass maker is unknown, but the figurative panels of American opalescent glass set in the lower and upper lights of the two-story Gothic windows are as tall as the sanctuary. This window shows *Ruth Gleaning*, below, after a painting by Lajo Bruck (1846-1910), and the *Good Shepherd*, above, after Bernard Plockhorst (1825-1907), a Munich-trained painter. The Gothic canopies at the head of the window are a delicate and light contrast to the sober academic weight of the figural images.

The three windows of the south wall (*above*) of St. Mary's-on-the-Highlands show the *Resurrection* in the center and, to the left, *Christ Blessing the Children*, the two earliest Mayer of Munich windows, both made in 1900. The Jacoby window of *The Two Crowns* is on the right.

The Two Crowns window, *also pictured page 62*, was adapted from a painting by Sir Francis Bernard Dicksee. The window, installed in 1919, is a memorial to the men of St. Mary's who served in World War I. The maker is the Jacoby Art Glass Studio of St. Louis. Jacoby finished the windows in the nave of the church in the style begun by Franz Mayer of Munich who completed the first windows done for the church.

The south wall of the sanctuary of Highlands United Methodist Church frames a display of stained glass. The architectural motifs of the glass, classical arches and Corinthian pilasters, form a weighty arch and platform for *Christ as the Great Counselor*. The architecture in the glass echoes that of the wall. The wall has a boldly projecting entablature which breaks forward on either side of the central window to carry flaming urns beneath the central dome.

Set into the entrance façade of Sixteenth Street Baptist Church is the window of the *Crucified Christ* who is black. This window was the gift of the people of Wales as a memorial of the bombing of the church on 15 September 1963 which killed four young girls and injured other members of the congregation. The window was designed and executed by the Welsh artist John Petts and installed in 1965.

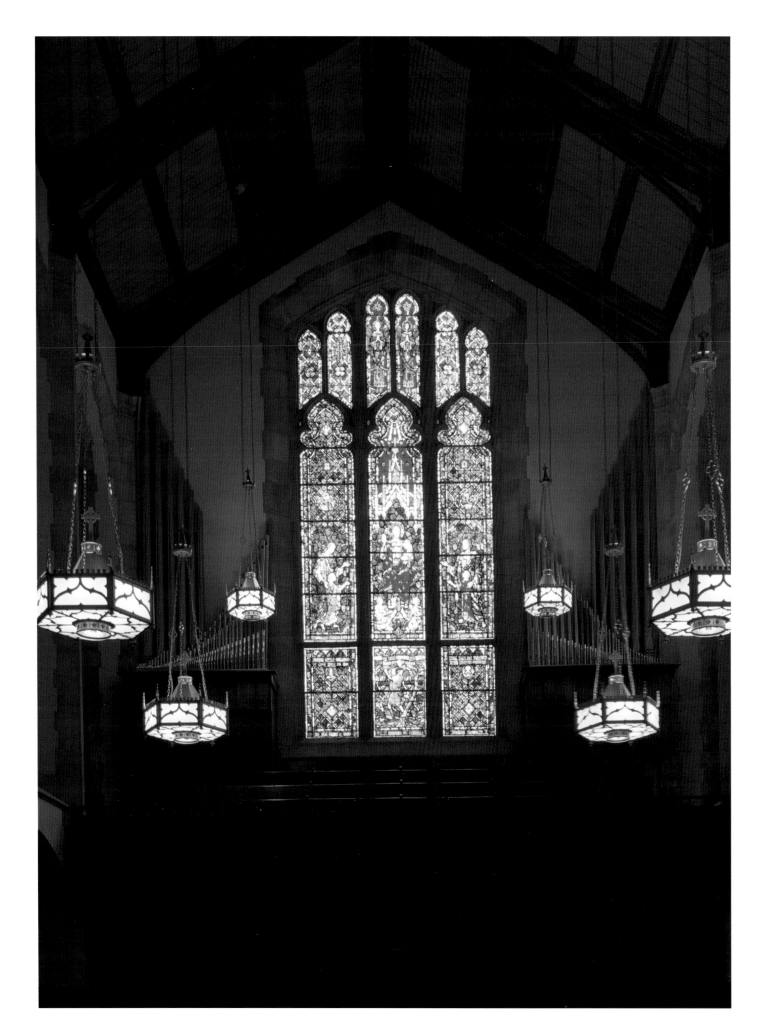

Independent Presbyterian Church

Highland Avenue at Thirty-first Street South
Built: 1922, 1925-1926
Architects: Warren and Knight; Miller and Martin,
Associated Architects (1922)
Warren, Knight & Davis (1925-1926)

Independent Presbyterian Church is the best Neo-Gothic church design in Birmingham. The basement level of the sanctuary and the education wing on Highland Avenue were completed in October 1922. The church was finished in 1925 and 1926, but the stained glass windows by the D'Ascenzo Studios of Philadelphia were installed from 1938 to 1960.

The sources of the design of the church are fourteenth- and fifteenth-century English Perpendicular Gothic, but the external copper spire is more French than English, and the internal planning of the sanctuary is more that of a Gothic collegiate hall than a church.

The earliest stained glass window is the one in the entrance wall, *left*. The subject is *Christ Blessing Little Children*. The dominant colors are an intense saturate blue and a strong dark red. The blue is the ground, and its choice emulates the blue in the glass of Chartres Cathedral. The smallness of the individual pieces of glass follows Gothic practice also, but there is more and stronger yellow here than that which appears at Chartres.

Viewed from Highland Avenue, *above*, the mass of the main sanctuary dominates the boulevard frontage while the cloister-front education wing extends to the right, sheltered by trees.

The side view of the sanctuary shows its compact verticality. The steep slope of the roof and the spire at the crossing of nave and transept heighten this theme. The scale of the stonework is human, the blocks not immeasurably big. Thus the height can seem intimate. The compact length and galleries in the nave and transepts make this a preaching church. The pulpit is taller than the altar and nearly as wide. Independent Presbyterian well represents the compromise of American Protestant church architecture which, in the 1920s, partly accepted and adapted medieval liturgical planning of a central aisle and dominant altar as well as medieval architectural forms.

Visible from across Rushton Park, *above*, are additions to the left of the sanctuary, including a new Education Building and side entrance (1993, KPS Group, architect) made after a major fire in 1992.

The interior of the sanctuary, *right,* looking toward the altar and choir gallery above, features a window representing the *Te Deum* flanked by mosaics of the four evangelists, Matthew, Mark, Luke and John. Both window and mosaics are the work of D'Ascenzo Studios and were installed in 1947.

St. Andrew's Episcopal Church

Eleventh Avenue at Twelfth Street
Built: 1913
Architect: Marriott and Joy

The red-brown stone of this Neo-Gothic building was quarried on Red Mountain. St. Andrew's Episcopal Church was designed by John M. Marriott (1879-1958), who practiced architecture in Birmingham for just three years, from 1913 to 1916, before moving to Texas. The style is simplified English Perpendicular Gothic, but the surface rustication and emphatic drafting of the stone is more nineteenth-century than medieval. This is the church of a neighborhood, and the house next door (about 1910) gives some idea of the neighborhood character. Eugene Knight, one of the architects of Independent Presbyterian Church lived about two blocks further down the street and attended church at another neighborhood church, the Second Presbyterian (today the University of Alabama at Birmingham's Honors House), just down the hill from St. Andrew's. Across Twelfth Street, the former home of the Eleventh Avenue Methodist Church still stands.

The clever thickening of the central part of the entrance wall of St. Andrew's carries the bell gable at its apex, just strong and large enough for its single bell.

Third Presbyterian Church

Sixth Avenue South at Twenty-second Street
Built: 1902
Architect: Unknown

The Third Presbyterian Church is the replacement for the first wooden building which burned and left the poor congregation with no place to worship. The Reverend John ("Brother") Bryan, pastor of the church, would not incur debt to buy the land for the new building or to build it. Nonetheless, the building rose, though slowly and, in part, by the labor of the congregation. The church is simple Gothic in brick, wood, and terra cotta, an octagon with corner tower vestibules.

Holy Trinity-Holy Cross
Greek Orthodox Cathedral

Third Avenue South at Nineteenth Street
Built: 1949-1950, 1955
Architect: George P. Turner

This Neo-Byzantine building has a richly decorated interior. Its broad barrel vaults, multiple arches, and richly carved capitals evoke the multiple squared bays and rich, dense surface ornament of Middle-Byzantine architecture. Built from 1949 to 1950, it replaced the earlier Holy Trinity Church which since 1906 had used a Methodist church on the site. Holy Cross Church united with Holy Trinity in 1953, and the new church became the Greek Orthodox Cathedral of Alabama in 1972.

The interior of the nave, *above,* looking toward the iconastasis, shows the murals of the *Virgin and Child* in the apse vault, *Abraham and Sarah Entertaining Angels,* and the *Christ Pantocrater* in the vault. These were painted by Costa Lydakis of New York in 1955. Carvings over the main entrance, *left,* were designed by the architect.

Avondale United Methodist Church

Fortieth Street South at Fifth Avenue
Built: 1931
Architect: Miller and Martin

Avondale Methodist is the second church building of this congregation, replacing the first wooden building of 1887. The sanctuary and education building form an L-shaped plan with adjacent walls at a right angle. These enclose the street corner garden that continues the park across the street. The Education Wing was built before the sanctuary. This dramatic presentation of English Perpendicular Gothic in rough-face red brick and grey limestone was finished in 1931. The powerful mass of the great limestone entrance door is flanked by buttresses of limestone below, brick above, limestone capped. They frame the limestone tracery of the immense façade window above the door. The side windows, smaller and rectangular below, large and pointed above, lying in the same plane in their respective stories, suggest the balcony which, in fact, exists within.

South Avondale Baptist Church

Fourth Avenue South at Forty-first Street
Built: 1914-1916
Architect: James E. Green

South Avondale Baptist is a clever enclosure of an "Akron Plan" design in what appears to be a rectangular building with an Ionic façade and central dome. The building is really three-sided. The unseen wall is the curving rear of an auditorium which faces the pulpit in the right corner of the structure. Thus, the exterior front is an interior side. The two big, arched windows light the sides of the congregational space. This is a sophisticated exercise in fitting a nineteenth-century plan into an early twentieth-century, Neo-Palladian classical exterior. James E. Green (active 1914-1927) also designed Calvary Baptist Church, *page 81*, and Grace Episcopal Church in Birmingham, and was active as a church architect in the South. The congregation recently sold the church to the Alabama Baptist Association.

East Lake United Methodist Church

First Avenue South at Seventy-eighth Street
Built: 1945-1948
Architect: Turner and Batson

The tower of East Lake United Methodist Church rises above the East Lake Cemetery that fills much of the blocks in front of it in the photograph on the left. This third church building for an early Methodist congregation in an old suburb of Birmingham was the proudest achievement of its architect, George P. Turner (1896-1984), who was a member of the congregation and lived across the street from the church he designed.

Woodlawn United Methodist Church

First Avenue North at Fifty-fifth Street
Built: 1907, 1909-1912
Architect: unknown

Woodlawn United Methodist Church, *above,* is closer to downtown Birmingham than the church in East Lake. The name of the architect of the tall American Romanesque structure is unknown, but George Turner redesigned the entrance steps when First Avenue was widened. The church still dominates the center of Woodlawn, its tower visible some distance in each direction.

East Lake United Methodist Church

First Avenue South at Seventy-eighth Street
Built: 1945-1948
Architect: Turner and Batson

East Lake United Methodist Church is a great work of American architecture. Its tower is a distant presence among the comfortable houses of its early twentieth-century neighborhood. The severe Romanesque cliffs of its tall brick walls, striping stone voussoirs in the arches, and adorned diaper in brick and stone over the deep-arched entrance portal astonish the viewer and compel attention to each detail.

Pictured below are portraits of members of the church choir, which George Turner directed, as well as the architect's inventive wit. The detail is seen on the inner capital of the right jamb of the side door. The winged being in the outer capital has a body that ends in Ionic volutes and Corinthian acanthuses. This strange invention is probably Turner's own.

Ruhama Baptist Church

Second Avenue South at Seventy-ninth Street
Built: 1923-1926
Architect: William Leslie Welton

Two Baptist churches, Ruhama in East Lake, *below*, and Calvary in Fountain Heights, *right*, represent the 1920s expansion of old and growing congregations. These versions of the classical church building make major use of the classical orders and provide large spaces for growing congregations.

Ruhama Baptist is the fourth building for this congregation, which was founded in 1819. William L. Welton

(1874-1934) drew designs for the church complex in 1921. The Education Building was completed before the church, and the work was done in stages as money became available. Construction of the sanctuary began in 1925, and it was dedicated on 5 September 1926. This was the church of Howard College then in East Lake. Howard later moved to Homewood and became Samford University.

Macedonia Seventeenth Street Baptist Church

(Old Calvary Baptist Church)
1405 Thirteenth Avenue North
Built: 1922
Architect: James E. Green

Across the city, Calvary Baptist Church began in 1907 as the merger of Fountain Heights Baptist Church (originally Third Baptist, est. 1886) and North Highland Baptist Church (est. 1905). An education building was erected, but no sanctuary. The cornerstone of the present sanctuary was laid 1 July 1922. The architect was James E. Green, a member of the congregation. He was described in *The Birmingham News* on 1 July 1922 as "a church architect of South-wide reputation, having drawn plans for some of the largest churches in the South" and being "well recommended by the Baptist Sunday School Board, of Nashville, Tenn."

Ruhama survived the move of Howard College and is still an active Baptist congregation. Calvary grew and prospered until the 1950s, when it was the third largest Baptist congregation in the city. Then its people began to move to the new expanding suburbs, and they were replaced by black residents of the city, some of whom

had been displaced by highway construction. So Calvary closed its doors in 1965 and sold its property to the Macedonia Seventeenth Street Baptist Church founded in 1885 by black Baptists in this part of Birmingham.

Green's widely spaced four Corinthian columns are less correctly disposed than William Welton's six sparse Tuscan columns at Ruhama. Welton uses pilasters at the corners of the façade and down the flanks. Green's sanctuary is a simpler box outside, but it has a glorious Corinthian interior.

Welton's Education Building is far more controlled and contained in design than the tall, flat, multi-windowed front of the Education Building for Calvary, designed by N. O. Patterson, Baptist pastor and church architect, Patterson's work is also to be seen in the second Hunter Street Baptist Church.

Blessed Sacrament Catholic Church

1460 Pearson Avenue SW
Built: 1928-1930
Architect: John J. Carey and Paul Dowling, Mobile

Blessed Sacrament Church is one of the hidden glories of Birmingham church architecture. The parish was organized in 1911, and this is its second church. John J. Carey and Paul F. Dowling of Mobile designed and built the church from 1928 to 1930. The yellow brick and white limestone form smooth walls layered in planes and semicircular arches for doors and windows. These are essentially Italian Romanesque forms.

The three original altars in the main and side apses came from the Cathedral of the Immaculate Conception in Mobile and are said to have been made about 1850. The interior painted decoration was done by the Rambusch firm of New York in 1955. Adjustments to the liturgical requirements of the Second Vatican Council required removal of some rails and the provision of the new freestanding altar.

Sardis Baptist Church

(Old Hunter Street Baptist Church)
Fourth Court West at Seventeenth Street
Built: 1927-1929, second church
*   1956-1958, third church*
Architects: N. O Patterson, 1927-1929
*   Turner, Smith and Batson, 1956-1958*

Since its founding in 1908, Hunter Street Baptist Church has occupied three buildings at this site. Two of them are visible in the picture to the right. The twin towers and arcaded porch of the second church are in the center of this photograph. That building was designed by N. O. Patterson, who was called as pastor in 1927. The cornerstone is dated 1928. The plain brick building has Renaissance intentions in its Palladian façade window and the forms of the semicircular arches and cornice.

The third church overwhelms the second. The newer building was designed by Turner, Smith, and Batson in 1955 and built from 1956 to 1958. This is a superb exercise in modified Georgian, particularly good in steeple and entrance doorway and subtle in the delicate acanthus of the interior columns which carry short architraves that span the transverse-vaulted aisles.

Metropolitan C.M.E. Church

(Old St. Joseph's Catholic Church)
Avenue K at Sixteenth Street
Built: 1914
Architect: unknown

Before St. Joseph's Catholic Church was veneered in brick, clapboard siding extended the full height of walls and tower. The narrow porch had a pedimental roof just wide enough to cover the door and carried on box pilasters. The center light of the window over the door stepped higher than the sidelights. The dividing tracery and segmental heads of the side windows are unchanged, as are the classical console brackets which support the overhang of the steep tower roof. The interior of the church is its most remarkable aspect, despite the loss of the original stained glass. Slender wooden piers carry a skeletal roof frame which suggests a shallow central barrel vault. Extraordinary Gothic-cusped roundels are set in the framing over the aisles. This is adventurous, idiosyncratic, craftsman carpentry of the highest order. Unfortunately, we do not know who designed it. The Diocese of Mobile often supplied designs for Catholic churches built in this era. The church served Italian families in the former Little Italy Ensley neighborhood.

Ensley Baptist Church

Avenue E at Twenty-third Street
Built: 1928-1929
Architect: Philip S. Mewhinney

Philip S. Mewhinney (1889-1971) was born in Birmingham and educated at the Carnegie Institute of Technology, Pittsburgh, and the Atelier Thomas-Laloux, Paris. In his design of this church, exterior and interior are perfectly joined. Between the stair towers rises the street facade, a sweep of steps that rushes up between the three huge Tudor Gothic arches of the deep porch. The interior has breadth approaching depth, wrapped in balcony cliffs, walled in yellow, Gothic-framed light, covered in the dark beamed patches of the roof, and closed by the dark panelling of the rostrum and the solemn dignity of the choir and organ wall. This close-to-the-preacher room

seats 1,500 people and was said to be the second largest church in Birmingham when it was built. It has a gaunt, gathering, closing, luminous presence worth every penny of the $150,000 it cost to build, a burden of debt it took until 1946 to pay.

An unusual feature visible on the exterior, *left,* are the diagonal bands of masonry extending across front and side windows. These mark the rise of the stairs within that connect street floor public rooms with the main floor auditorium and balcony, *pictured above.*

Glossary

acanthus. A plant, common in Greece, with scalloped leaves used as an ornament in capitals of columns in the Corinthian and Composite orders of classical architecture.

American Renaissance. The version of Beaux-Arts Classicism which revived the styles of Italian Renaissance architecture in the United States, especially from about 1890 to about 1930.

American Romanesque. Romanesque Revival style architecture in the United States during the 1870s and 1980s, deriving from the architecture of H. H. Richardson.

arcade, arcading. A row of arches supported by columns or piers.

arch. A curved structure spanning an opening and made of wedge-shaped blocks.

architrave. The lintel or beam from one column or pier to the next; also, the lowest of the three main divisions of a classical entablature.

ark. Cupboard in which the rolls of the law are kept in a synagogue.

balustrade. A row of short posts (balusters).

Beaux-Arts Classicism. The richly elaborate classical style practiced by the nineteenth-century Ecole des Beaux-Arts in France, by American architects trained there, and by those architects influenced by the school and its practitioners.

bema. In Early Christian churches, a raised platform for the clergy. In synagogues, the elevated place from which the Pentateuch and Torah are read, often now close to the ark.

boss. An ornamental projecting block.

Byzantine. An architectural style developed from ancient Roman models in the Christian East, beginning in the fourth century and continuing to the sixteenth. Many church buildings have domes and central, often cross-shaped plans. The sources of ornament are classical; their use is flatter and approaching abstract patterning.

canopy. A hood or covering projected or hung over a special location such as a pulpit, altar, or tomb.

capital. The top part of a column or pilaster, having one of a number of conventional ornamental forms and supporting the entablature.

Churrigueresque. A late Baroque architectural style developed in Spain from 1700 to 1750 by the three Churriguera brothers. Richly and complexly ornamented, the style was much imitated in Spanish America.

Classical. The general name for the successive related styles of ancient Greek and Roman architecture and the imitations and developments from it during the Italian Renaissance and later periods. Classical architecture uses the Doric, Ionic, Corinthian, Tuscan, and Composite orders.

clerestory. The upper walls of the central space of a church or other building, above lower lateral spaces and pierced by windows to give direct light to the central space.

Colonial. The style of architecture in the colonies of a mother country derived from that homeland, as in the thirteen English colonies of North America derived from the English Queen Anne and Georgian styles or in the Spanish colonies of Central and South America derived from Spanish Hispano-Moresque and Churrigueresque styles.

Colonial Revival. A late nineteenth- and twentieth-century use of the forms of Colonial architecture. The term normally means American Colonial Revival.

console. A vertical monumental bracket with a scrolled profile, usually higher than its projection from the wall and supporting something above it

Corinthian. The name of the most elaborately ornamented of the three classical Greek orders. Acanthus leaves surround its column capitals.

cornice. The topmost of the three divisions of a classical entablature; also the projecting ornamented ledge crowning a wall or building. The molding at the top of a wall or building, crowning it.

course. In a wall, a continuous layer of masonry units such as stone, brick, or tile.

cove ceiling. A flat ceiling having a concave molding of considerable height to connect it to the walls below.

diaper, diaper patterns, diaper work. Surface decoration of repeated patterns like lozenges or squares.

Doric. The name of the earliest and simplest of the three classical Greek architectural orders.

eclectic. A term used to describe an architectural style which chooses and combines elements from many styles or successive stages of one style.

English Perpendicular Gothic. See Perpendicular Gothic.

entablature. The upper part of one of the classical orders consisting, from bottom to top, of architrave, frieze, and cornice.

façade. The front or main face of a building.

finial. An ornament, often with leafy decoration, at the top of a gable, pinnacle, or spire.

gable. The triangular end of a building.

gallery. A partial upper story or mezzanine, often supported on columns, at the sides or rear of an interior space which overlooks it.

Gothic. An architectural style and system of construction in Western Europe from 1140 to about 1550. Elements include pointed arches, stone skeletal construction, rib vaults, and thin or transparent window walls.

Gothic Revival. The style which, from the mid-eighteenth century to the present, reuses the decorative and structural forms of the medieval Gothic style. *See Neo-Gothic.*

hammerbeam. A wooden-framed roof-framing structure with projecting horizontal brackets (the hammerbeams) extending at the top of the side walls to carry vertical posts and arched braces to a transverse collar beam beneath the apex of the roof.

helix. A spiral form, also an ornamental volute. That beneath the abacus of a Corinthian capital.

hexastyle. Having six columns in a portico.

High Victorian Gothic. A phase of the Gothic Revival practiced from 1850 to 1880. The style minimizes archaeological exactness and emphasizes polychromy.

hip roof, also hipped roof. A roof having sloping sides and ends.

iconastasis. In Byzantine churches, a screen or wall which separates the altar area from the nave and is adorned with icons (holy images).

Ionic. The second in development of the three classical Greek orders of architecture. The column has a base. The column capital is largely formed by the double outward and downward curve of the volute.

jamb. The vertical surface forming the side of an archway, door, or window.

liturgical. Having to do with and architecturally responsive to the liturgy, that is the services of the church, especially the Mass or Holy Eucharist.

Lombard, Lombard Romanesque. The eleventh century early Romanesque style of the Lombardy region of North Italy in and around Como.

lozenge. A diamond shape.

masonry. Stonework, brickwork, tile work, concrete block work built by masons

Middle Byzantine. The period of Byzantine architecture extending between the ninth and twelfth centuries.

mosaic. A decoration or picture made by laying small pieces of different-colored stones or gilded glass into a bed of cement.

nave. In a church, the central higher space between flanking aisles, or this central space and the aisles together, or any space intended for occupation by the people rather than the clergy. Many Protestants use the terms sanctuary or auditorium to describe this space.

Neo-Classicism. The revived and correcting use of the styles of ancient Classical architecture from about 1750 to about 1840 and again from about 1900 to about 1930. Inspired by new knowledge of Greek Classical architecture after 1750 and new archaeological discoveries from 1750 onward. A reaction to the free Classicism of the late Renaissance and the Baroque and the eclectic Classicism of the nineteenth century.

Neo-Gothic. Architecture, in the United States chiefly of the twentieth century, reviving the Gothic style in forms which are historically and archaeologically more correct than those of the earlier Gothic Revival. The ensemble may still be eclectic.

Neo-Palladian. The eighteenth- to twentieth-century revival of the classical style developed by the Italian architect Andrea Palladio (1508-1580).

Neo-Romanesque. A style continuing the historicism of the Romanesque Revival into the twentieth century, simplifying forms and decorations.

opalescent. Reflecting an iridescent light.

order, orders. (1) In Classical architecture or its revivals a column with base (except for Greek Doric), shaft, capital, and entablature, with decoration and proportion according to the rules of one of the Classical orders, Doric, Tuscan, Ionic, Corinthian, or Composite. (2) In Romanesque and Gothic an arched opening built as several stepwise- receding parallel layers.

palette. A particular range, quality, or use of colors.

Palladian, Palladianism. The Classical architectural style of the Italian architect Andrea Palladio (1508-1580), developed in his buildings and publications based on ancient Roman models.

patera. A circular or oval ornament in classical architecture in friezes and in the rosette form in the Corinthian capital.

Perpendicular Gothic. The last stage of Gothic architectural style in England, from about 1335 to 1550, having vertical emphasis in the tracery of windows and the decorative carved paneling in stone and wooden forms.

pier. A freestanding support for an arch or lintel, square or composite in section, thicker than a column.

pilaster. A shallow pier attached to a wall, often decorated to look like a classical column.

pinnacle. A tapering turret-like termination in Gothic architecture, usually finished like a steep pyramid.

polychromy. The decoration of architecture with many colors.

portico. A roofed space, often with columns, which covers and partly encloses the entrance to a building, especially to a classical temple or a structure copied from the temple form.

Rayonnant. The Gothic style in France between about 1230 and about 1350, characterized by radiating geometric arrangements of tracery in the windows.

Renaissance. The name of the style of architecture in Italy from about 1420 to about 1550. Its sources were the known remains of Roman Classical architecture.

reredos. The stone or wood screen behind an altar, usually adorned with painting, sculpture, or both.

Romanesque. The style of European architecture from the tenth to the thirteenth centuries used before the Gothic. Buildings have thick masonry walls, often in multi-planed relief; semicircular arches for arcades, doors, and windows; and a strong sense of spatial division.

Romanesque Revival. A style from 1840 to 1900 of usually monochromatic stone or brick buildings using semicircular arches structurally and decoratively. Usually has towers with polygonal roofs.

roundel. A small circular niche, panel, opening, or window.

rusticated masonry. Stone with a rough face, laid in courses with deep joints.

sanctuary. In a traditionally planned Christian church, the area immediately around the principal altar. In many American Protestant churches, the name for the whole of the interior space used for worship.

segmental arch. A segment of a circle drawn from a center below the springing of the arch.

Spanish Colonial Revival. An architectural style reviving the forms of architecture in Colonial Spanish America. It flourished from 1911 to 1940. Stylistic features include: arcaded porches, red-tiled roofs, often hipped, stucco-finished walls, wrought iron grills, and decorative low relief carved or terracotta ornament.

tabernacle. A roofed or canopied covering, especially a miniature stone building formed by columns and gabled roof which adorns the buttresses of Gothic buildings. A closed shrine-cupboard for the Eucharistic elements of bread and wine in a Christian church or for the Torah in a synagogue.

terracotta. A hard-burned glazed or unglazed clay, plain or ornamented, used in building.

tetrastyle. Having four columns in a portico.

tie rod. A metal rod under tension, used to hold parts of a building together.

tracery. The stone dividers in a Gothic window or similar opening, usually arranged in a geometrically ordered branch like pattern. Wooden tracery is sometimes used in Gothic Revival buildings.

transept. The transverse arms or wings of a church which has a cross- or T-shaped plan.

Tuscan. The ancient Roman form of the Doric order. The column has a base and the shaft is usually not fluted.

Victorian. A general term for the multiplicity of architectural styles, sometimes mixed with one another, which were in use during the reign of Queen Victoria, especially between about 1840 and about 1890.

Victorian Gothic. See High Victorian Gothic.

volute. A form with a downward-curving scroll at each end used in the Ionic capital.

voussoir. One of the wedge-shaped blocks forming an arch or vault.

Index

Double dates indicate the beginnings and ends of lives and construction.